WEEKLY PRAYER JOURNAL

WRITTEN & DESIGNED BY SHALANA FRISBY

COPYRIGHT 2018. ALL RIGHTS RESERVED.

WWW.123JOURNALIT.COM

Don't forget to grab your bonus freebies today!
WWW.123JOURNALIT.COM / FREEBIES
SCRIPTURE FLASHCARDS - BIBLE READING PROMPTS - JOURNALING PAGES

More information at: www.123journalit.com

First Printing: 2018
1 2 3 Journal It Publishing

Pocketbook 6x9-in. Format Size
Weekly Prayer Journal Series

THIS JOURNAL
BELONGS TO

_____

MY PRAYER NOTES FOR THE WEEK OF _____ TO _____

MONDAY:

TUESDAY:

WEDNESDAY:

THURSDAY:

FRIDAY:

SATURDAY:

SUNDAY:

ANSWERED PRAYERS & THINGS I'M THANKFUL FOR THIS WEEK:

MY PRAYER NOTES FOR THE WEEK OF _____ TO _____

MONDAY:

TUESDAY:

WEDNESDAY:

THURSDAY:

FRIDAY:

SATURDAY:

SUNDAY:

ANSWERED PRAYERS & THINGS I'M THANKFUL FOR THIS WEEK:

MY PRAYER NOTES FOR THE WEEK OF _____ TO _____

MONDAY:

TUESDAY:

WEDNESDAY:

THURSDAY:

FRIDAY:

SATURDAY:

SUNDAY:

ANSWERED PRAYERS & THINGS I'M THANKFUL FOR THIS WEEK:

MY PRAYER NOTES FOR THE WEEK OF _____ TO _____

MONDAY:

TUESDAY:

WEDNESDAY:

THURSDAY:

FRIDAY:

SATURDAY:

SUNDAY:

ANSWERED PRAYERS & THINGS I'M THANKFUL FOR THIS WEEK:

_____
_____
_____
_____
_____
_____
_____

MY PRAYER NOTES FOR THE WEEK OF _____ TO _____

MONDAY:

TUESDAY:

WEDNESDAY:

THURSDAY:

FRIDAY:

SATURDAY:

SUNDAY:

ANSWERED PRAYERS & THINGS I'M THANKFUL FOR THIS WEEK:

MY PRAYER NOTES FOR THE WEEK OF _____ TO _____

MONDAY:

TUESDAY:

WEDNESDAY:

THURSDAY:

FRIDAY:

- -
- -
- -
- -

SATURDAY:

- -
- -
- -
- -

SUNDAY:

- -
- -
- -
- -

ANSWERED PRAYERS & THINGS I'M THANKFUL FOR THIS WEEK:

_____

_____

_____

_____

_____

_____

MY PRAYER NOTES FOR THE WEEK OF _____ TO _____

MONDAY:

TUESDAY:

WEDNESDAY:

THURSDAY:

FRIDAY:

SATURDAY:

SUNDAY:

ANSWERED PRAYERS & THINGS I'M THANKFUL FOR THIS WEEK:

MY PRAYER NOTES FOR THE WEEK OF _____ TO _____

MONDAY:

TUESDAY:

WEDNESDAY:

THURSDAY:

FRIDAY:

SATURDAY:

SUNDAY:

ANSWERED PRAYERS & THINGS I'M THANKFUL FOR THIS WEEK:

MY PRAYER NOTES FOR THE WEEK OF _____ TO _____

MONDAY:

TUESDAY:

WEDNESDAY:

THURSDAY:

FRIDAY:

SATURDAY:

SUNDAY:

ANSWERED PRAYERS & THINGS I'M THANKFUL FOR THIS WEEK:

MY PRAYER NOTES FOR THE WEEK OF _____ TO _____

MONDAY:

TUESDAY:

WEDNESDAY:

THURSDAY:

FRIDAY:

SATURDAY:

SUNDAY:

ANSWERED PRAYERS & THINGS I'M THANKFUL FOR THIS WEEK:

MY PRAYER NOTES FOR THE WEEK OF _____ TO _____

MONDAY:

TUESDAY:

WEDNESDAY:

THURSDAY:

FRIDAY:

SATURDAY:

SUNDAY:

ANSWERED PRAYERS & THINGS I'M THANKFUL FOR THIS WEEK:

_____
_____
_____
_____
_____
_____

MY PRAYER NOTES FOR THE WEEK OF _____ TO _____

MONDAY:

TUESDAY:

WEDNESDAY:

THURSDAY:

FRIDAY:

SATURDAY:

SUNDAY:

ANSWERED PRAYERS & THINGS I'M THANKFUL FOR THIS WEEK:

MY PRAYER NOTES FOR THE WEEK OF _____ TO _____

MONDAY:

TUESDAY:

WEDNESDAY:

THURSDAY:

FRIDAY:

SATURDAY:

SUNDAY:

ANSWERED PRAYERS & THINGS I'M THANKFUL FOR THIS WEEK:

MY PRAYER NOTES FOR THE WEEK OF _____ TO _____

MONDAY:

TUESDAY:

WEDNESDAY:

THURSDAY:

FRIDAY:

SATURDAY:

SUNDAY:

ANSWERED PRAYERS & THINGS I'M THANKFUL FOR THIS WEEK:

MY PRAYER NOTES FOR THE WEEK OF _____ TO _____

MONDAY:

TUESDAY:

WEDNESDAY:

THURSDAY:

FRIDAY:

SATURDAY:

SUNDAY:

ANSWERED PRAYERS & THINGS I'M THANKFUL FOR THIS WEEK:

MY PRAYER NOTES FOR THE WEEK OF _____ TO _____

MONDAY:

TUESDAY:

WEDNESDAY:

THURSDAY:

FRIDAY:

SATURDAY:

SUNDAY:

ANSWERED PRAYERS & THINGS I'M THANKFUL FOR THIS WEEK:

MY PRAYER NOTES FOR THE WEEK OF _____ TO _____

MONDAY:

TUESDAY:

WEDNESDAY:

THURSDAY:

FRIDAY:

SATURDAY:

SUNDAY:

ANSWERED PRAYERS & THINGS I'M THANKFUL FOR THIS WEEK:

MY PRAYER NOTES FOR THE WEEK OF _____ TO _____

MONDAY:

TUESDAY:

WEDNESDAY:

THURSDAY:

FRIDAY:

SATURDAY:

SUNDAY:

ANSWERED PRAYERS & THINGS I'M THANKFUL FOR THIS WEEK:

MY PRAYER NOTES FOR THE WEEK OF _____ TO _____

MONDAY:

TUESDAY:

WEDNESDAY:

THURSDAY:

FRIDAY:

SATURDAY:

SUNDAY:

ANSWERED PRAYERS & THINGS I'M THANKFUL FOR THIS WEEK:

MY PRAYER NOTES FOR THE WEEK OF _____ TO _____

MONDAY:

TUESDAY:

WEDNESDAY:

THURSDAY:

FRIDAY:

SATURDAY:

SUNDAY:

ANSWERED PRAYERS & THINGS I'M THANKFUL FOR THIS WEEK:

MY PRAYER NOTES FOR THE WEEK OF _____ TO _____

MONDAY:

TUESDAY:

WEDNESDAY:

THURSDAY:

FRIDAY:

SATURDAY:

SUNDAY:

ANSWERED PRAYERS & THINGS I'M THANKFUL FOR THIS WEEK:

MY PRAYER NOTES FOR THE WEEK OF _____ TO _____

MONDAY:

TUESDAY:

WEDNESDAY:

THURSDAY:

FRIDAY:

SATURDAY:

SUNDAY:

ANSWERED PRAYERS & THINGS I'M THANKFUL FOR THIS WEEK:

_____

_____

_____

_____

_____

_____

_____

MY PRAYER NOTES FOR THE WEEK OF _____ TO _____

MONDAY:

TUESDAY:

WEDNESDAY:

THURSDAY:

FRIDAY:

SATURDAY:

SUNDAY:

ANSWERED PRAYERS & THINGS I'M THANKFUL FOR THIS WEEK:

MY PRAYER NOTES FOR THE WEEK OF _____ TO _____

MONDAY:

TUESDAY:

WEDNESDAY:

THURSDAY:

FRIDAY:

SATURDAY:

SUNDAY:

ANSWERED PRAYERS & THINGS I'M THANKFUL FOR THIS WEEK:

MY PRAYER NOTES FOR THE WEEK OF _____ TO _____

MONDAY:

TUESDAY:

WEDNESDAY:

THURSDAY:

FRIDAY:

SATURDAY:

SUNDAY:

ANSWERED PRAYERS & THINGS I'M THANKFUL FOR THIS WEEK:

MY PRAYER NOTES FOR THE WEEK OF _____ TO _____

MONDAY:

TUESDAY:

WEDNESDAY:

THURSDAY:

FRIDAY:

SATURDAY:

SUNDAY:

ANSWERED PRAYERS & THINGS I'M THANKFUL FOR THIS WEEK:

MY PRAYER NOTES FOR THE WEEK OF _____ TO _____

MONDAY:

TUESDAY:

WEDNESDAY:

THURSDAY:

FRIDAY:

SATURDAY:

SUNDAY:

ANSWERED PRAYERS & THINGS I'M THANKFUL FOR THIS WEEK:

MY PRAYER NOTES FOR THE WEEK OF _____ TO _____

MONDAY:

TUESDAY:

WEDNESDAY:

THURSDAY:

FRIDAY:

SATURDAY:

SUNDAY:

ANSWERED PRAYERS & THINGS I'M THANKFUL FOR THIS WEEK:

MY PRAYER NOTES FOR THE WEEK OF _____ TO _____

MONDAY:

TUESDAY:

WEDNESDAY:

THURSDAY:

FRIDAY:

SATURDAY:

SUNDAY:

ANSWERED PRAYERS & THINGS I'M THANKFUL FOR THIS WEEK:

MY PRAYER NOTES FOR THE WEEK OF _____ TO _____

MONDAY:

- -
- -
- -
- -

TUESDAY:

- -
- -
- -
- -

WEDNESDAY:

- -
- -
- -
- -

THURSDAY:

- -
- -
- -
- -

FRIDAY:

- -
- -
- -
- -

SATURDAY:

- -
- -
- -
- -

SUNDAY:

- -
- -
- -
- -

ANSWERED PRAYERS & THINGS I'M THANKFUL FOR THIS WEEK:

MY PRAYER NOTES FOR THE WEEK OF _____ TO _____

MONDAY:

TUESDAY:

WEDNESDAY:

THURSDAY:

FRIDAY:

SATURDAY:

SUNDAY:

ANSWERED PRAYERS & THINGS I'M THANKFUL FOR THIS WEEK:

MY PRAYER NOTES FOR THE WEEK OF _____ TO _____

MONDAY:

TUESDAY:

WEDNESDAY:

THURSDAY:

FRIDAY:

SATURDAY:

SUNDAY:

ANSWERED PRAYERS & THINGS I'M THANKFUL FOR THIS WEEK:

MY PRAYER NOTES FOR THE WEEK OF _____ TO _____

MONDAY:

TUESDAY:

WEDNESDAY:

THURSDAY:

FRIDAY:

SATURDAY:

SUNDAY:

ANSWERED PRAYERS & THINGS I'M THANKFUL FOR THIS WEEK:

MY PRAYER NOTES FOR THE WEEK OF _____ TO _____

MONDAY:

TUESDAY:

WEDNESDAY:

THURSDAY:

FRIDAY:

- -
- -
- -
- -

SATURDAY:

- -
- -
- -
- -

SUNDAY:

- -
- -
- -
- -

ANSWERED PRAYERS & THINGS I'M THANKFUL FOR THIS WEEK:

MY PRAYER NOTES FOR THE WEEK OF _____ TO _____

MONDAY:

TUESDAY:

WEDNESDAY:

THURSDAY:

FRIDAY:

SATURDAY:

SUNDAY:

ANSWERED PRAYERS & THINGS I'M THANKFUL FOR THIS WEEK:

MY PRAYER NOTES FOR THE WEEK OF _____ TO _____

MONDAY:

TUESDAY:

WEDNESDAY:

THURSDAY:

FRIDAY:

SATURDAY:

SUNDAY:

ANSWERED PRAYERS & THINGS I'M THANKFUL FOR THIS WEEK:

MY PRAYER NOTES FOR THE WEEK OF _____ TO _____

MONDAY:

TUESDAY:

WEDNESDAY:

THURSDAY:

FRIDAY:

SATURDAY:

SUNDAY:

ANSWERED PRAYERS & THINGS I'M THANKFUL FOR THIS WEEK:

MY PRAYER NOTES FOR THE WEEK OF _____ TO _____

MONDAY:

TUESDAY:

WEDNESDAY:

THURSDAY:

FRIDAY:

- -
- -
- -
- -

SATURDAY:

- -
- -
- -
- -

SUNDAY:

- -
- -
- -
- -

ANSWERED PRAYERS & THINGS I'M THANKFUL FOR THIS WEEK:

MY PRAYER NOTES FOR THE WEEK OF _____ TO _____

MONDAY:

TUESDAY:

WEDNESDAY:

THURSDAY:

FRIDAY:

SATURDAY:

SUNDAY:

ANSWERED PRAYERS & THINGS I'M THANKFUL FOR THIS WEEK:

_____

_____

_____

_____

_____

_____

_____

MY PRAYER NOTES FOR THE WEEK OF _____ TO _____

MONDAY:

TUESDAY:

WEDNESDAY:

THURSDAY:

FRIDAY:

SATURDAY:

SUNDAY:

ANSWERED PRAYERS & THINGS I'M THANKFUL FOR THIS WEEK:

MY PRAYER NOTES FOR THE WEEK OF _____ TO _____

MONDAY:

TUESDAY:

WEDNESDAY:

THURSDAY:

FRIDAY:

- -
- -
- -
- -

SATURDAY:

- -
- -
- -
- -

SUNDAY:

- -
- -
- -
- -

ANSWERED PRAYERS & THINGS I'M THANKFUL FOR THIS WEEK:

MY PRAYER NOTES FOR THE WEEK OF _____ TO _____

MONDAY:

TUESDAY:

WEDNESDAY:

THURSDAY:

FRIDAY:

SATURDAY:

SUNDAY:

ANSWERED PRAYERS & THINGS I'M THANKFUL FOR THIS WEEK:

MY PRAYER NOTES FOR THE WEEK OF _____ TO _____

MONDAY:

TUESDAY:

WEDNESDAY:

THURSDAY:

FRIDAY:

- -
- -
- -
- -

SATURDAY:

- -
- -
- -
- -

SUNDAY:

- -
- -
- -
- -

ANSWERED PRAYERS & THINGS I'M THANKFUL FOR THIS WEEK:

MY PRAYER NOTES FOR THE WEEK OF _____ TO _____

MONDAY:

TUESDAY:

WEDNESDAY:

THURSDAY:

FRIDAY:

SATURDAY:

SUNDAY:

ANSWERED PRAYERS & THINGS I'M THANKFUL FOR THIS WEEK:

MY PRAYER NOTES FOR THE WEEK OF _____ TO _____

MONDAY:

TUESDAY:

WEDNESDAY:

THURSDAY:

FRIDAY:

SATURDAY:

SUNDAY:

ANSWERED PRAYERS & THINGS I'M THANKFUL FOR THIS WEEK:

MY PRAYER NOTES FOR THE WEEK OF _____ TO _____

MONDAY:

TUESDAY:

WEDNESDAY:

THURSDAY:

FRIDAY:

SATURDAY:

SUNDAY:

ANSWERED PRAYERS & THINGS I'M THANKFUL FOR THIS WEEK:

MY PRAYER NOTES FOR THE WEEK OF _____ TO _____

MONDAY:

TUESDAY:

WEDNESDAY:

THURSDAY:

FRIDAY:

SATURDAY:

SUNDAY:

ANSWERED PRAYERS & THINGS I'M THANKFUL FOR THIS WEEK:

MY PRAYER NOTES FOR THE WEEK OF _____ TO _____

MONDAY:

TUESDAY:

WEDNESDAY:

THURSDAY:

FRIDAY:

SATURDAY:

SUNDAY:

ANSWERED PRAYERS & THINGS I'M THANKFUL FOR THIS WEEK:

MY PRAYER NOTES FOR THE WEEK OF _____ TO _____

MONDAY:

TUESDAY:

WEDNESDAY:

THURSDAY:

FRIDAY:

SATURDAY:

SUNDAY:

ANSWERED PRAYERS & THINGS I'M THANKFUL FOR THIS WEEK:

MY PRAYER NOTES FOR THE WEEK OF _____ TO _____

MONDAY:

TUESDAY:

WEDNESDAY:

THURSDAY:

FRIDAY:

SATURDAY:

SUNDAY:

ANSWERED PRAYERS & THINGS I'M THANKFUL FOR THIS WEEK:

MY PRAYER NOTES FOR THE WEEK OF _____ TO _____

MONDAY:

TUESDAY:

WEDNESDAY:

THURSDAY:

FRIDAY:

SATURDAY:

SUNDAY:

ANSWERED PRAYERS & THINGS I'M THANKFUL FOR THIS WEEK:

MY PRAYER NOTES FOR THE WEEK OF _____ TO _____

MONDAY:

TUESDAY:

WEDNESDAY:

THURSDAY:

FRIDAY:

SATURDAY:

SUNDAY:

ANSWERED PRAYERS & THINGS I'M THANKFUL FOR THIS WEEK:

57740017R00067

Made in the USA
Columbia, SC
12 May 2019